T0086552

Ultimate Bass Exercises

"Over 700 easy step-by-step exercises for finger building, based on the 24 possible fingering combinations"

by Max Palermo

Thanks to Patrizia for her unconditional encouragement and valuable support and to Ron Middlebrook and all at Centerstream Publications for all their efforts in realizing this project.

Special thanks to my teacher Attilio Zanchi.

This book is dedicated, in loving memory, to my grandfather Domenico.

ISBN-13: 978-1-57424-208-9
ISBN-10: 1-57424-208-3
SAN-683-8022

Contents

Introduction

The aim of this two-workbook set is to provide bass players with a wide range of step-by-step exercises to improve the finger physical dexterity, in terms of strength, independence, agility and velocity.

This is an important goal to reach for a musician in order to free his own musical personality.

I would therefore advise you to practice these exercises daily (two or three finger combinations per day), starting quite slowly and gradually increasing the metronome (or drum machine) speed.

While playing, always keep a clean and well-defined sound together with a good rhythmic feel.

Last but not least: keep on studying the harmonic-melodic-rhythmic issues of your instrument and the different musical styles, so that your technical improvements make it possible to put into practice what is in your mind and what your body can feel!

Enjoy your work!

How to use this book

The exercises in this book are based on all the 24 possible fingering combinations listed in the table below, where each number refers to the corresponding finger of the left hand as indicated in the legend.

1 2 3 4	2 1 3 4	3 1 2 4	4 1 2 3
1 2 4 3	2 1 4 3	3 1 4 2	4 1 3 2
1 3 2 4	2 3 1 4	3 2 1 4	4 2 1 3
1 3 4 2	2 3 4 1	3 2 4 1	4 2 3 1
1 4 2 3	2 4 1 3	3 4 1 2	4 3 1 2
1 4 3 2	2 4 3 1	3 4 2 1	4 3 2 1

1 = index finger
2 = middle finger
3 = ring finger
4 = little finger

Part One

Exercises on

Adjacent strings

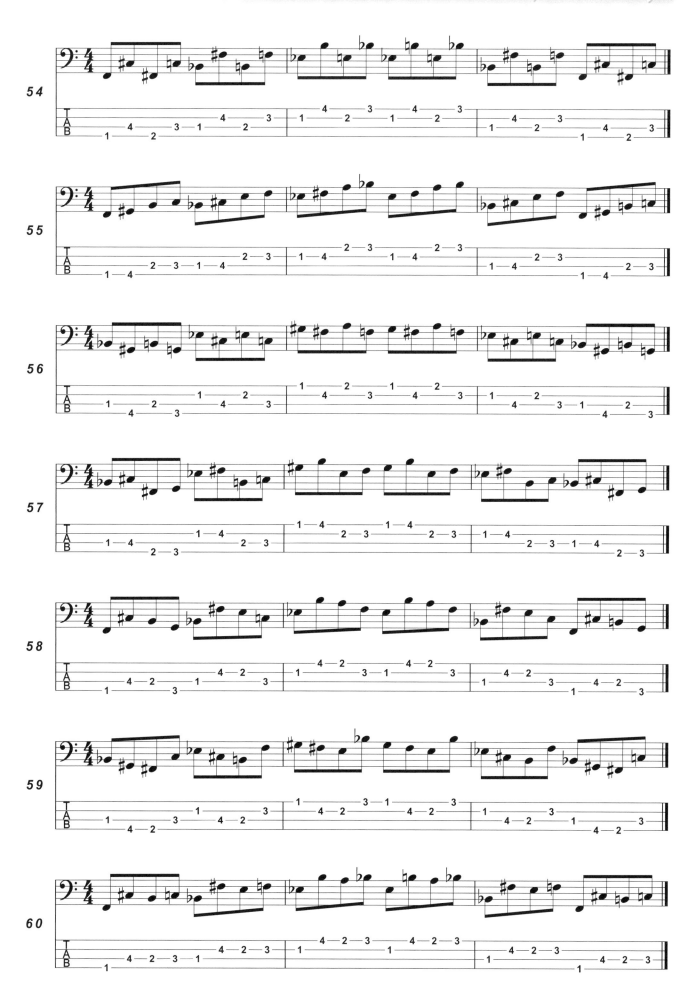

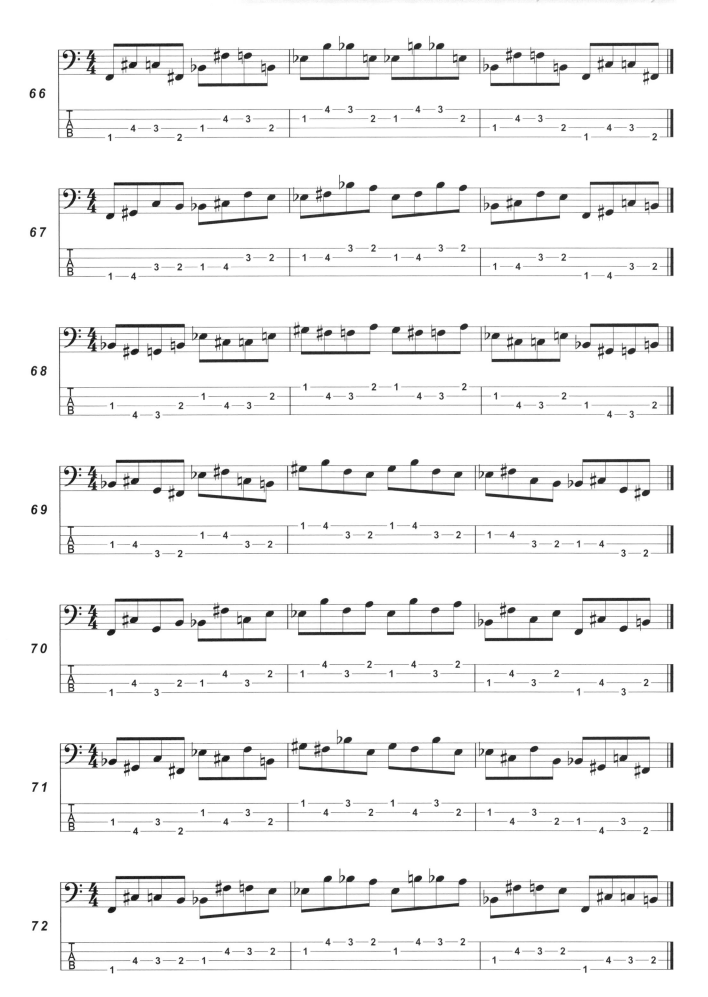

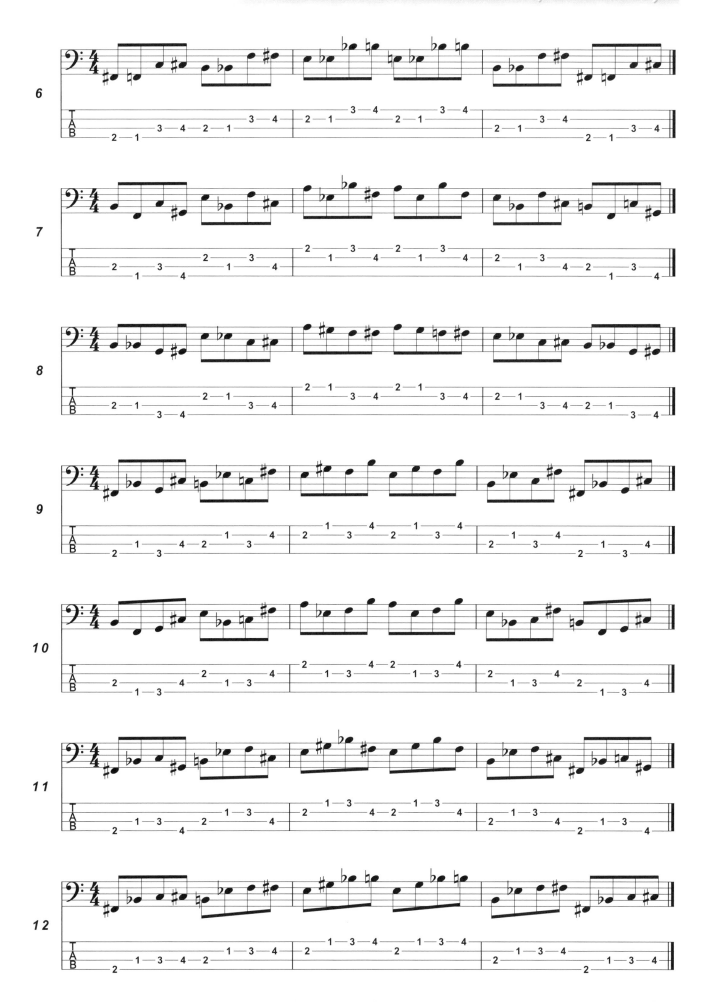

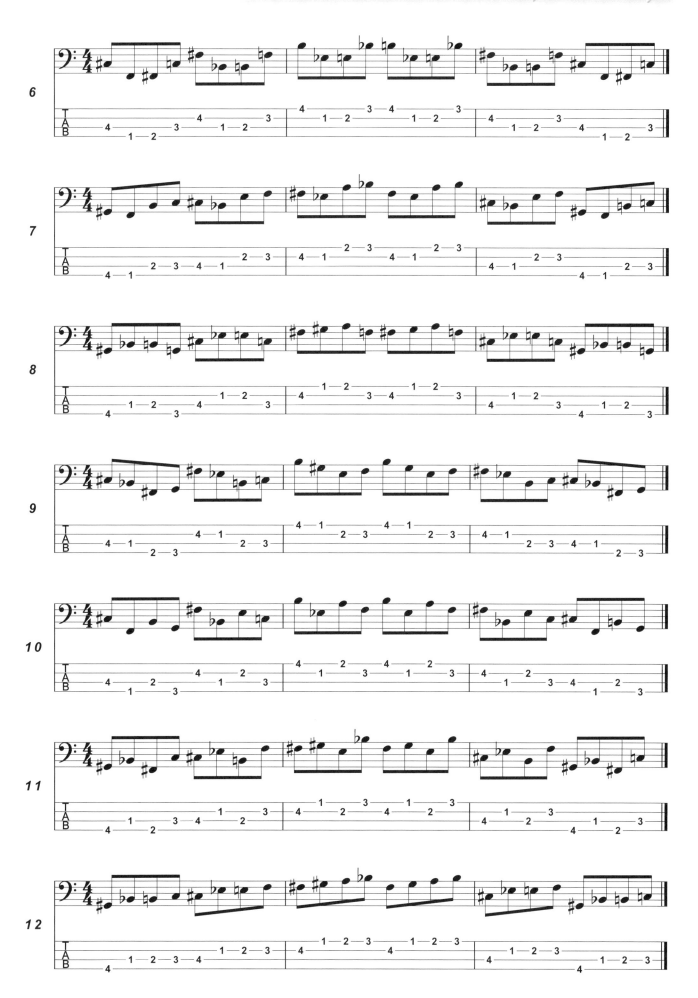

13 *Fingers 4 1 3 2 4 1 3 2   4 1 3 2 etc.*

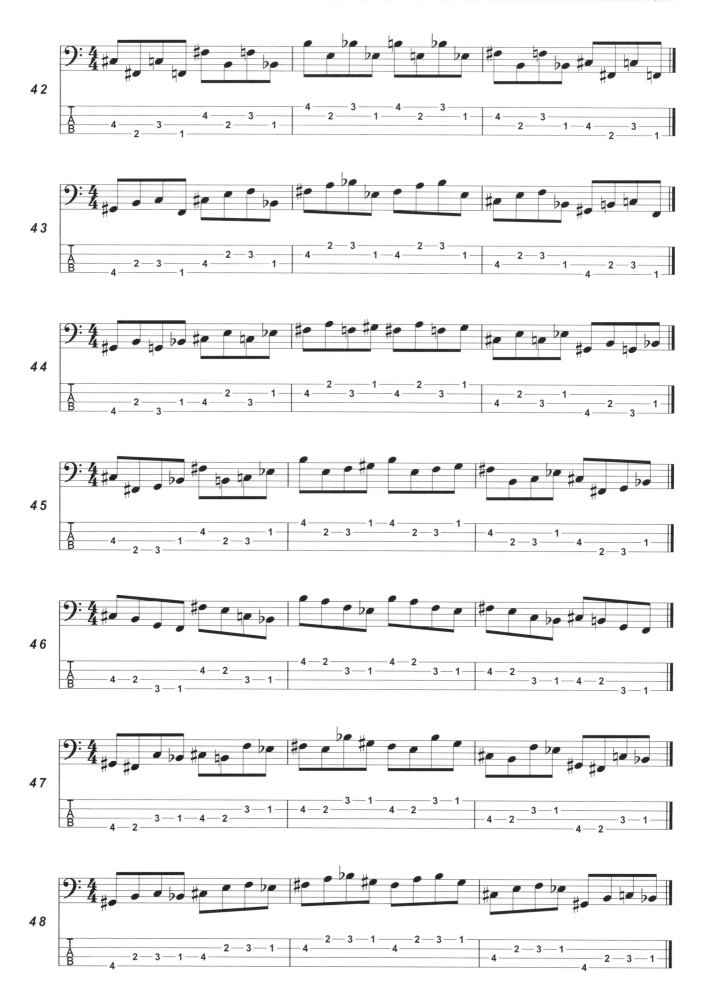

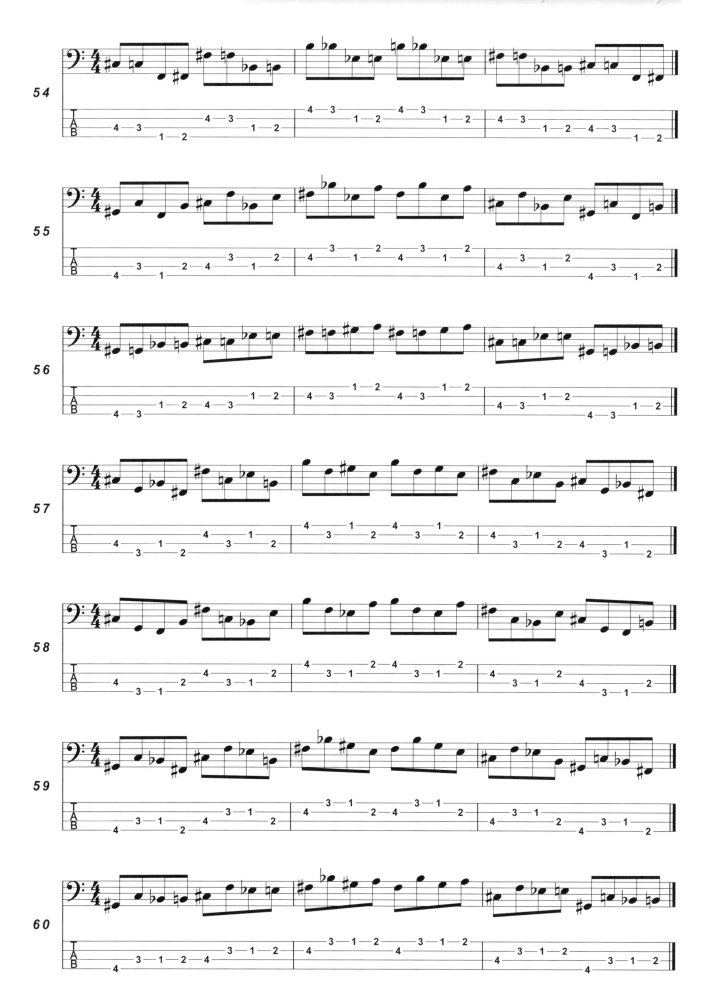

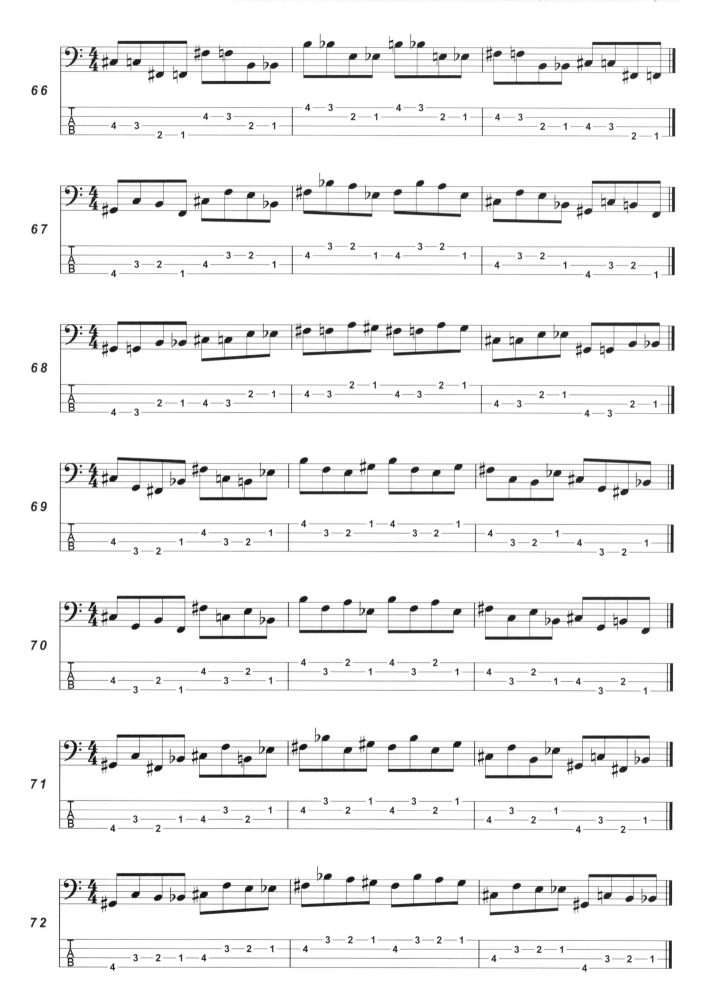

Part Two

Additional exercises

Along the neck

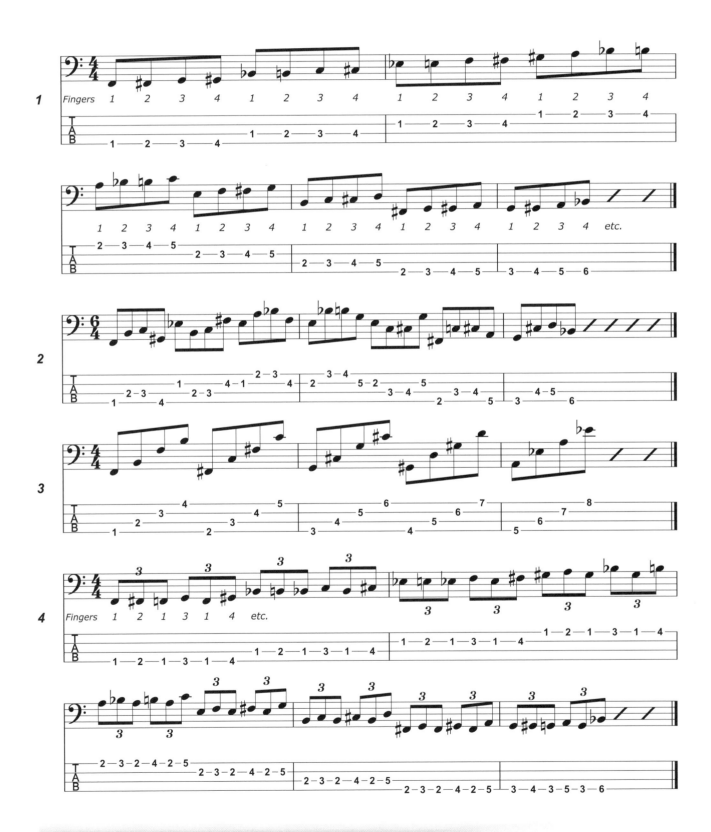

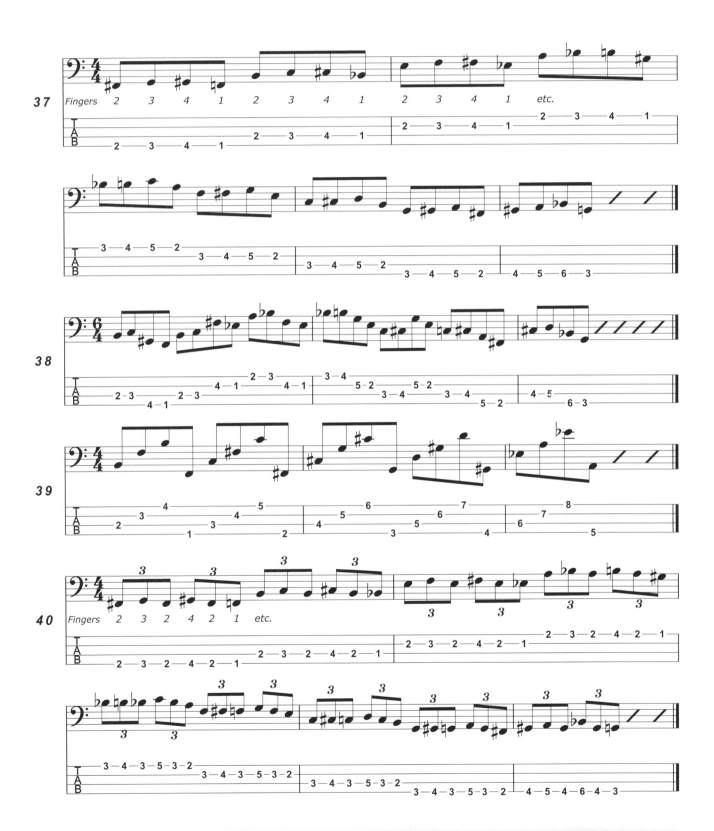

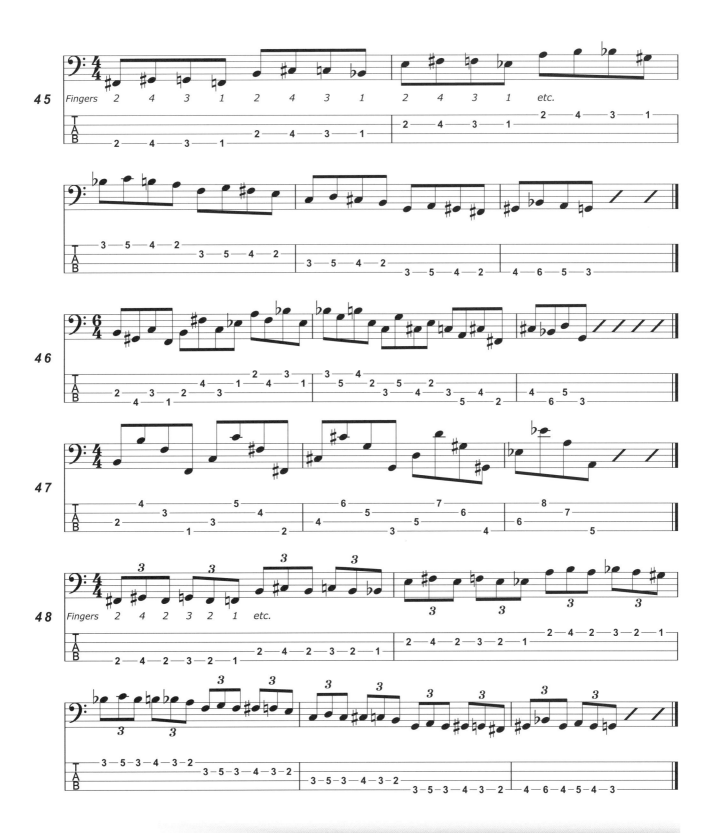

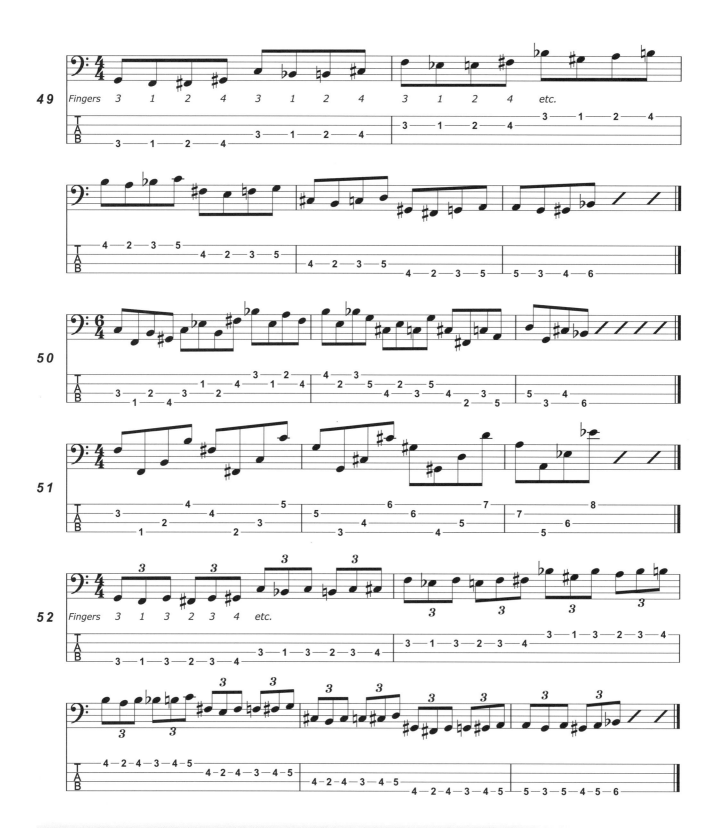

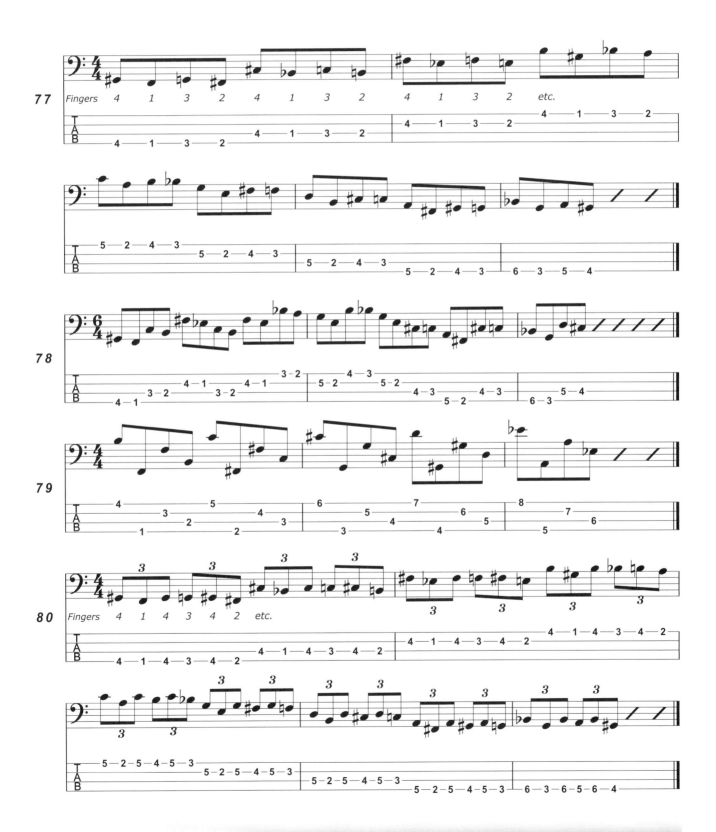

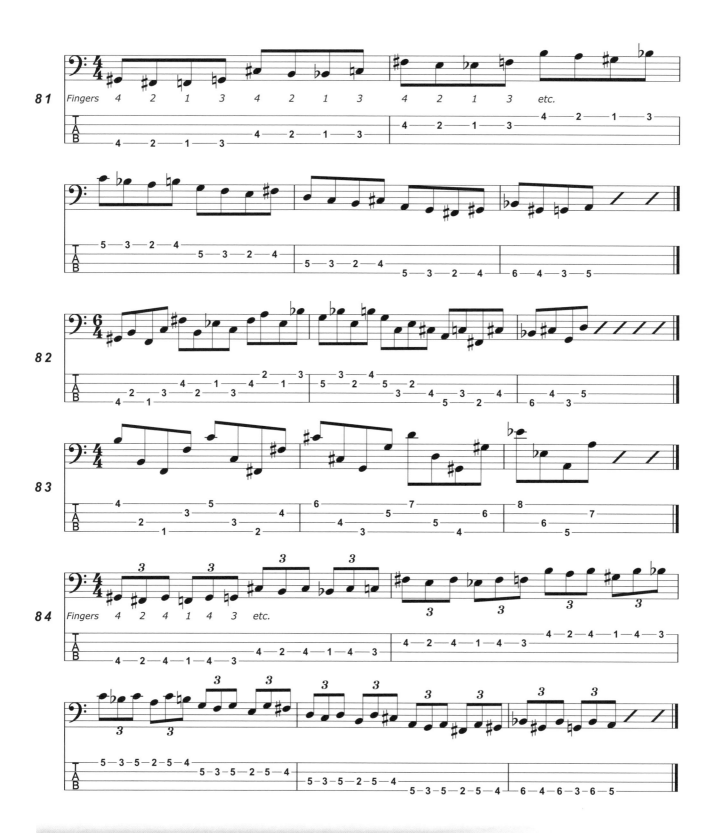

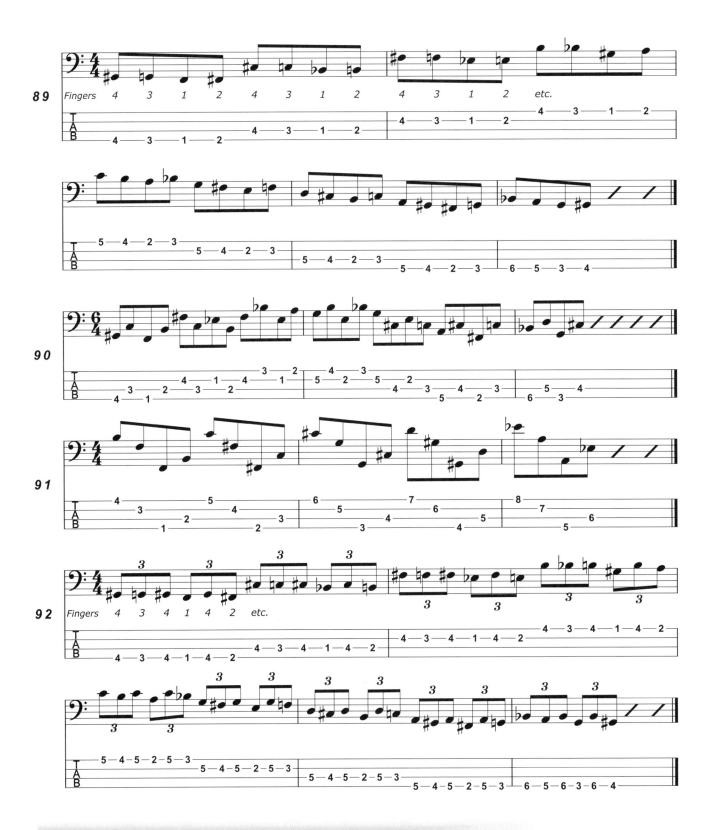

Max Palermo

Part One

Exercises for

Moving across strings

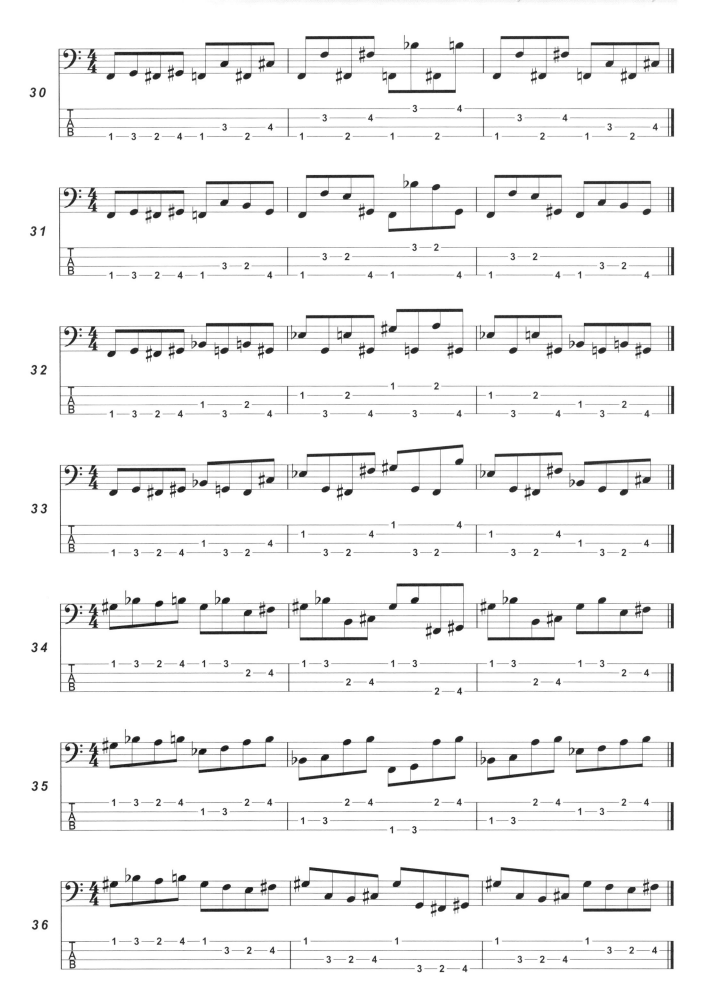

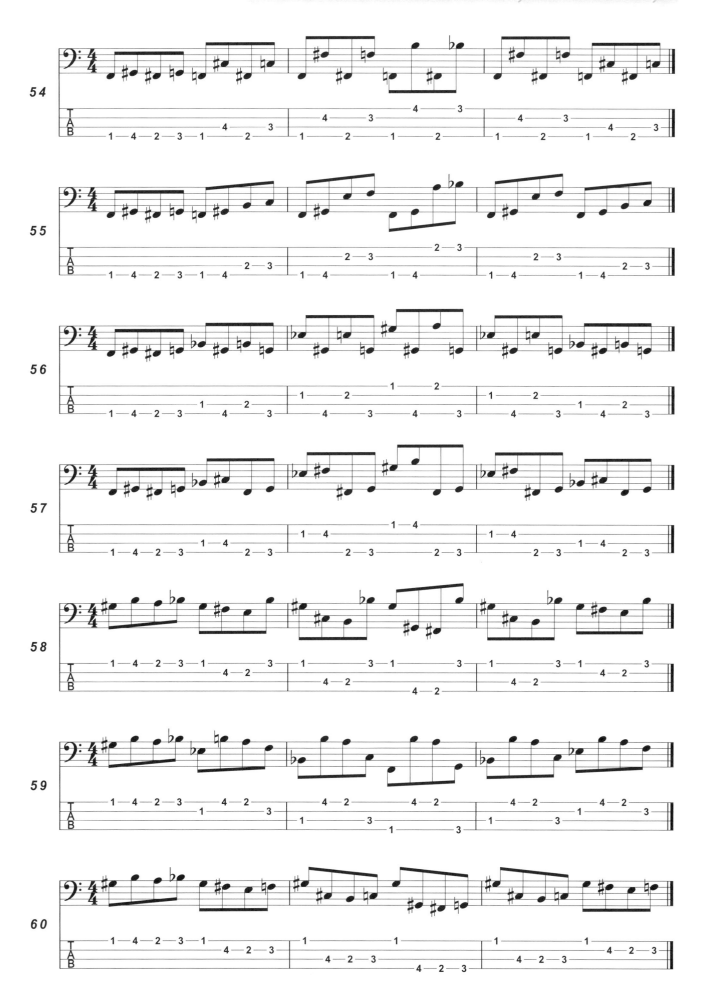

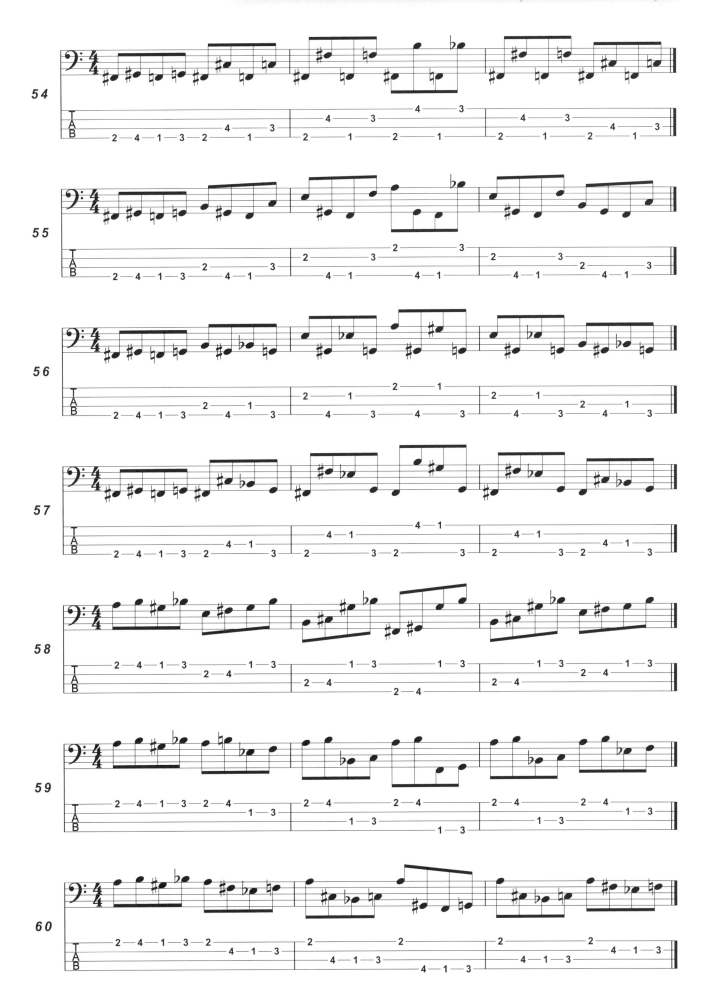

Ultimate Bass Exercises

Ultimate Bass Exercises

Part Two

Stretching

Exercises

Three Fingers

Three Fingers

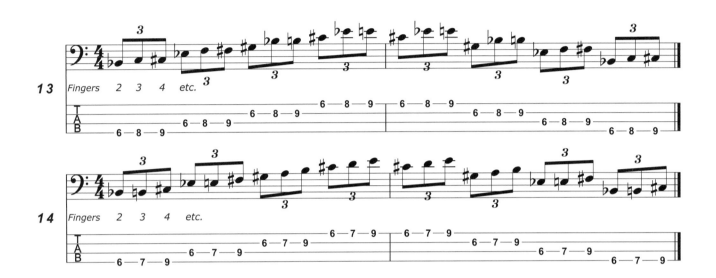